Right Lane
Must Exit

Right Lane Must Exit

ERIC SWAN

THE ERIC SWAN COMPANY
SAN JOSE, CALIFORNIA

First edition, February 2019.

ISBN 9781795724913

Published by The Eric Swan Company

Printed in the United States of America

TABLE OF CONTENTS

*This book is dedicated to my sons
Noah and Ethan Swan.*

Remember that **love** is the greatest energy force we can
wield and always share it graciously and openly for who and
what you **love**. Be fearless and always remember that you are a
gift and imperfectly perfect.
Love your Dad.

Acknowledgment

To everyone that put up with me during my younger years. Mom and Dad, Veronica, the City of Hollister, and of course myself. Karen for supporting the book, and Stephanie for being a great editor. Without any of you this book would not be possible.

INTRODUCTION

Right lane must exit is a simple book that will explain the importance of self-awareness that defines connection, and the place we all have in the World. The World has patterns and if we are still, we can see them a little more clearly. The Title refers to the thought of if you are to travel on your intended lane you will naturally have to exit your old thoughts, feelings, and behaviors.

Right lane must exit is a leadership and business book revolving around the exciting world of weddings and interpersonal relationships.

Connection

"What The Fuck Tom? Can't you read the BEO? All *"my"* servers are here in *"your"* kitchen because you didn't fucking read the event order correctly! Now every plate is coming back undercooked!"

As I stood with the Executive Chef of a full-service luxury brand hotel in the middle of the kitchen right after I walked in and threw an improperly cooked prime rib meal for a wedding right at him as I was screaming like a Banshee. How exciting right?... Wrong! This is all too common and it was one of the many examples of what a *bad* leader I was. As I think back on moments like this, I am conflicted at times with feelings of both pride and embarrassment because of the confusion that comes with the monster and the pressure to make things happen at all costs with weddings and events. With over 3000 weddings and close to 50,000 events managed over the years, at the time of writing this book, I have come to understand a piece of my destiny, and why I'm writing this.

We do what we are taught. But hospitality, as an industry, has forgotten who they are, and what they stand for. They have forgotten how to lead, and build leaders. I felt like the new baby that was predestined to have character flaws and gifts, and nothing I did was going to change the force that created me and the way my life was going to go on a journey to create a change for my sons. The last thing I want or desire is to ever have them work for an asshole like me. I hope this book creates and inspires 'old way' leaders to change, and gives new leaders the courage to be great leaders of change. Now how did that kitchen brawl end? Tom asked me to hold on so he could grab his boxing gloves from his office so we could go outside and proceed like grown ass men. Lucky, we had our staff whose emotions didn't get the best of them to control two dopamine addicts with raging egos.

Connection and authenticity, which Tom and I had outside of the hotel, would have prevented us from behaving this way if we felt we had great leaders and felt safe in our choices and even in our mistakes. But our learned behavior was to blame others and protect our job security at all costs, even at the expense of our friends and more importantly ourselves.

Authentic

(NEVER FORGET TO BE YOURSELF, BUT SOMETIMES YOU WILL.)

In events, we have been culturally conditioned to believe that a guest, meeting planner or bride is always right. I'm not promoting disagreement or defending what is often the solution, but we have forgotten how to allow our employees and our customers to live authentically. And we have forgotten that, at a basic level, we are just truly human.

We need to retrain the industry as a whole that we, in fact, control nothing, and the mere fact that we believe that we can control thoughts, emotions, and ultimate behaviors is scary. Every day in business we do absolutely everything to ensure the outcome of our actions with complete confidence. However, living authentically will not only allow us to accept that we can't control anything, but in that release of pressure, we can be kinder people to each other. That's a dream of mine that one day brides and wedding planners will agree that the day we co-create is going to be done from the intention of *love* and we can have acceptance for the negative things that happen out of our control.

I remember so many events where the very same thing happened. The family and the couple wanted me to be superman, and just fix it or make something happen that was totally out of my control, nor my responsibility. Here are just a few things that can and will always happen at weddings and events.

I have experienced all of them:

- The wedding venue is sold out for your wedding day
- The church is not available for your date
- Invitations you desire have been discontinued
- That bonus you expected to help cover expenses was not as big as you planed
- Hired DJ called to say that he wasn't showing up because his truck with his equipment broke down
- Having food enough for 100 people when an additional unexpected 70 people show up
- Flight delays for family
- Hotel rooms sold out
- Flowers freeze overnight in the cooler
- Power goes out during the reception

I can think of thousands of other moments and situations that can happen that are out of our control, yet we think as the hired professional and/or leaders we take full responsibility for these universal moments. I continue to get blown away at how long we have continued this behavior without having anyone stop and mention this is not mentally healthy and needs to change.

So I have committed to making a vow that I will only and always have a conversation with my couples and family members if they are participating that no matter what happens or fails to happen, don't let anything take the joy and bliss of the one day that should be filled with pure *love* and acceptance.

In making sure that I have this conversation, I can come with compassion in the moments of high pressure and calmly express the need to breathe and let the universe create the wedding day that is destined and will create effortlessly.

Being Authentic: Genuine

Not many words have a one-word definition, but being authentic allows for the purest form of oneself and because true acceptance of one's self, and self-*love* we can non-compromisingly truly be a genuine person. I also know that being a genuine person means being a gracious human being. But it takes courage and it takes the breaking down of one's ego to truly find the vulnerable self that can have compassion in a world where so many people and relationships exist in fear.

Marriage and couples that *love* each other selflessly and with vulnerability have the ability to be 100 true to themselves and to each other. The manifestation of pure unconditional never dying *love* is the commitment to the bond as husband and wife. *Love* is a feeling and marriage is a choice. We tend to forget or have that backward today.

We live in a time that promotes living without feelings. Weddings are not planned because a bride just said, it's a choice and I think I'm going to say yes to the next man that makes me his wife. It's a feeling, and feelings are created inside our mind, not because of anything else.

So remember that weddings are choices created because of emotion and the emotion of *love*. It may seem simple and even elementary, but there are a number of broken homes and lives because of the confusion of their feelings and the commitment to each other. Unfortunately, you do have the very cynical bitches and man-haters that marry just for money and the control of a man. Those are just not in the universe of this book and the fuck with them anyway! Argh, I know! They still need *love* too!

With any creative person, and I believe that we are organically programmed to be creative creatures, self-doubt comes with a process of growth and it becomes easier to allow yourself to be transparent and constantly progressing. I find it amazing how unaware I was in the first thirty years of my life and how loss and pain thankfully opened my mind, heart, and soul to now experience a life filled with compassion and *love*.

Being authentic is the only way that one can make a connection to oneself and to people that have the courage to be authentic. This allows for genuine connection and great positive relationships. We have been culturally conditioned to believe with a certain amount of expectations in how to live, and how others should live in order for acceptance. I will express how with these expectations create loneliness and fear in us.

Parents have the purest of *love* for their children, and no matter what mistakes they make, parents are able to have compassion knowing that their children are not perfect. However, why is it so hard for us to have that same unconditional bond in our work, immediate family, and with our friends? I also know that because of the lack of care for someone it's even harder to have compassion and understanding for people we don't have relationships with, constantly judging them for not acting how we expect that they should.

We have lost our humanity, and it's time we get back to the basics of what keeps us connected. Let's start with understanding how we are made of energy, the same energy that created the moon and the stars. I'm a huge fan of Superhero stories because the messages always follow a particular pattern that I can't deny. Identity and purpose are what the heroes struggle with. Batman, Superman, Ironman, and Spiderman are the clearest creative stories about the fear of not being accepted because of a special gift and the courage they had, in the end, to be true to the destiny that comes with the gifts they all possess.

I believe that now, more than ever, we are becoming people with a higher level of depression and anxiety because of our culture's expectations are not in our best interest of ourselves. When we have the courage to live the life that we truly desire we can be genuine and have compassion for those that do not have the courage and are consumed with depression, anxiety, and of course fear. Fear and *love* are the only motivators, and when you can see the patterns of how they each motivate someone, the ability to have compassion or to have connection becomes easy. That compassion and connection makes it easier for us to be kinder people.

Weddings have progressed in many ways, not many of them have the uncreative and dry dinner plates, or the cheesy disc jockey playing *celebration* and *we are family anymore*. With the growth of the quality of the consumer impact and desire to validate the *love* of a couple by the amount of entrée selections or the enormous amount of uneaten cake, the connection and the presence of pure *love* have been put on the back burner. Having the loss from the intention in gathering the closest friends and family in the presence of pure *love* has created the couples to be guided by the current wedding catalog trends, and the crazy hybrid flowers that are growing that season. What the industry is experiencing is an enormous outrage in Bridezillas, and the expectation that whatever they want at all cost, they shall be granted. I have seen too many brides that have been unhappy with the littlest of uncontrollable factors; to the day being completely ruined because a picture that she thought looked horrible, devastated her. With this precedent of behavior, marriages are failing because the new wives are slowly building up resentment for not being treated like a princess that she did during the courting stage of the relationship and onto the wedding day shenanigans.

Passion

(DO WHAT YOU *LOVE*, ALWAYS.)

Will Smith has a great story about how he and his brother had to build a brick wall for their father. They saw how big the wall needed to be and the anxiety started to worry and fill them with negativity. But then their dad told them to stop thinking about the finished wall, but concentrate on making sure they lay every brick perfectly. And sooner than later they would have built a perfect brick wall. It's the same as how you eat an elephant. One bite at a time!

What I know to be true is if we live a life that consists of waking up at 5:00am to grab our shitty cup of coffee in the same pajamas and sitting in the dusty living room, thinking about if we really want to get ready and go to work or say fuck it and grab a smoke and head to the beach and not think about anything ever again. By the time Saturday comes around, we are already late for the next social media experiment or the sale on the new electronic device that we really can't even afford anyway to dust on a lazy Saturday morning.

We are always trying to find our next superficial fix of dopamine because we have a fear of being successful or unsuccessful and are working at jobs that we are not happy at and will never be satisfied because of the lack of fulfillment in our daily lives. I know it's scary but as I am sitting here in the dark writing this chapter on passion, I realize it should be a great chapter because I need to express the value in the sacrifices needed to make the life I want. I need to emphasize that passion in order to inspire others to follow dreams and create the life they imagine.

I don't have a whole lot of experience working at a job I hated because of what the actual job was. I was lucky enough to always be working in the food and beverage industry, and it came naturally because it's in my blood. My father was a hotel professional for many luxury hotels, and my mother is a baker and decorator for her own bakery, and worked for many bakeries in her life prior to that.

When the time came for me to move out of the home I grew up in and start my own family, I moved to Las Vegas and started my own hospitality career. I was not unhappy with the work, but I was unhappy with the leaders. They forgot how to build confidence in teamwork, how to trust the process and, they forgot that people make mistakes daily. My passion for food, events, *love*, and positive energy is the reason I wake up every morning ready to conquer the day. That is what matters above all. It is just *today*.

I know how we can easily get consumed with the thoughts of what the future is going to look like, and what this job may or may not provide for me in a few years. If I were to just keep showing that I am capable of more, maybe my boss would see the effort and give me a raise, or a promotion.

Well, I'm telling you that this is no way to live. This behavior exists only with exhaustion the presence of self-doubt. When we are able to take control of our passion and recognizing who we are and how we are perceived to the outside world, we can have the courage to only make choices that are in the best interest of what our desires are. It is too common today to see fathers and husbands that miss family gatherings, or are coming home stressed from staying at work later than they truly wanted because of the fear that is in the lack of job security.

The universe will and has always provided for our basic needs. It may not provide you the beachfront property and the ability to be independently wealthy, because you are making choices that are blocking those things for you to receive. And the way you move out of the way is to have trust that living with passion is key to all the things that you desire. And true desire is what you're going to receive if you think you want a beachfront property, but your authentic desires are to have an apartment in an urban city, you will be guided to the apartment in the city. So knowing who you are and what your true desires are is important to living passionately and with *love*.

My favorite moments are when I hear stories of perseverance and living for your passion above all else.

Sylvester Stallone is one of my favorite actors, and it's not because of his pure talent as an actor because we know that he is not the most talented. But he has something that not very many celebrities have, and that is *heart!* When he wrote Rocky the movie, he was homeless and he had to sell his dog for a $20 bill. Imagine the amount of sacrifice that he had to make in order for him to let go of his best friend, and possibly only friend. When the part for Rocky Balboa was being cast, he felt that he would be the only one that could tell the story of this underdog. It turns out that he was right, and look at the legacy that he has created from living a life of non-compromising integrity and having the heart to never give up or stop moving for a cause because of a challenge.

Robert Downey Jr. was a hot mess in the 1980's and into the 1990's consumed with past mistakes, and a drug habit that became his identity. Trying to get back into the movie blockbusters, he at some point made a choice to do and live how he wanted, not being afraid to be himself. And because of his ability to be a great performer, and an amazing actor, he locked *Iron Man* and no one better could have even tried to be as naturally witty, charming playboy hero than Mr. Downey. From that moment he became the highest paid actors in the 2010's.

Moses was a Hebrew and was raised as an Egyptian son of the Pharaoh, yet he had the courage to sacrifice himself for the equality of his people. When Moses led the Hebrews over the Red Sea there are reports that say it was from 850,000,000 to 2.5 million Hebrews. This man took his life and dedicated it to the passion of being a leader, and for those enslaved by power.

Martin Luther King Jr. is one of the most honored men of the modern world. He was a southern black preacher who showed how *love* and having compassion for those who live in fear can and will continue to create movements that leave legacies to be remembered and be grateful for still today. He was able to gather over 250,000 people for his "I have a dream" speech on August 28th, 1963. He was able to do that without Twitter, Facebook, Instagram or a marketing agency -just by living with passion about equality.

Oprah Winfrey is the first and only billionaire black woman in the world. Her passion for inspiring people to live with *love* and believing in themselves and to follow their dreams has changed the lives of millions. She started as a poor black girl who was told she was unfit for TV. But her *heart* and *passion* allowed her to create her own TV show and now her *own* network.

All of these people have had difficulties and moments when they looked in the mirror or looked to a loved one and said, 'Is all this pain and sacrifice really worth it?'

I'm sure that many of them just said it would be so much easier if I just lived my little life with a loving family. But something in them knew that they had to push to create their dreams and to be leaders of whatever they knew was the *passion* inside leading them. So before you complain about the life you're living, be aware that every day is a choice. If we have the courage to allow the universe to guide us and our true desires, and our intentions are pure, we have the ability to create miracles. Living with fear and listening to the doubt from others can easily distract us if we allow it to have that much power. We then become victims to our life that we believe we can't control.

Baby steps… How do you eat an elephant? One bite at a time! Every day taking steps to allow ourselves to sit in the silence we can discover the answers to all of our problems. Recognizing what steps we should take and what steps are just not in the immediate time yet is important to having peace in living our life with passion.

Events have always been a passion of mine, and it is not about the flowers, the open bar, or even the food. Because of my passion for people and the connection that we desire from attending events is why I am passionate about them. I know that they can bring people together for a single cause and it allows us to have a common connection just because of the event and what its purpose is. One of the greatest memories I have was an event for C.O.D. Children of deaf adults. They conducted a general session with a keynote speaker and because of the small budget and the additional charges that they incurred during the convention they did not have the funds to pay for the needed sound system and technical support for the meeting. I told the event planner that I would be able to provide the house system, and because I didn't have much going on I could tech the room at no additional charge. Little did I know that my act of generosity and their appreciation, would lead to a donation b 3 times more than what the cost of the rentals would have been.

I was blessed with a gratuity just for doing something that they genuinely appreciated and felt that my passion for connection was genuine and transparent to them.

What's really funny about passion is once you communicate just a little about who you are and what you believe, even if you're not aware of it, people can see things inside of you when you can't see it yourself.

Having the courage to live with your passion means recognizing a few things -the importance of knowing what is contributing to your passion and what is not.

The other thing you need to identify is who you surround yourself with, and are they people that are living their passion. If you can't be vulnerable and allow the emotions to guild you on your journey, people and situations can be seen as untrusting or difficult that may not truly be as it is being seen.

Emotionally Available

(THE HUMAN NAVIGATION)

*Hate is not the first enemy of **love**. Fear is. It destroys your ability to trust.* –Unknown.

Emotions are the most powerful asset that we as creations have. They can tell us if we are in danger or in the presence of *love*. Having the ability to understand these emotions takes growth and experience. I have met teenagers that have grown up in difficult and broken homes that have more emotional intelligence than I had in my late 20's. What we need to understand is that Emotional Intelligence is the ability to be aware of yourself and how it allows you to have the delightful and decadent life we all deserve.

I am a huge fan of cinema and the ability for stories on screen are able to connect with our emotions based on what life experiences we have had or what we desire. Sylvester Stallone writes his movies with a simple pattern that is the journey of a man, meaning mankind. I have developed a simpler version of this process and it ultimately is the emotional growth of a man and the process of reaching our destiny.

Puppy: Innocence

When we are born, we are born from *love* and in the purest form of innocence. We don't have expectations or conditions on how we are to live or who we are to be, we just are. It's easy to see why children can say the darndest things and can walk up to a group of other children and just start playing without feeling judged or insecure. The time that we live in this stage of our life varies on our external environment and the people that we have in our life. I call this stage a puppy because it's very common for the term loyalty to be referred from the ability that no matter what we say or do if you continue to be in the presence of a dog, it will always have the purest of intentions and *love* you with unconditional loyalty. It's not the loyalty part that I *love* about the puppy but it's the reason why it is loyal. Dogs have the ability to stay true to who they are just like most creatures on the planet. Dogs don't ever think about the sadness of, "why am I not a seahorse or an eagle?" They understand that they are naturally selected to be a dog. And because it is able to have peace and accept that it is a dog, it can be in a constant state of peace. Having that peace, they are allowed to welcome us home with a wagging tail, and a tongue full of licking regardless of how long it has been and how we are feeling when they greet us.

Bear: Fear

Some point in our childhood we experience a moment of tragedy that could be our parent's divorce, the loss of a parent and, unfortunately, abuse. Because of these tragedies many will develop self-doubt that is consuming and causes a constant state of fear.

This is the stage of a man that most people live in and will remain in the longest if we don't have the courage to have self-forgiveness and to forgive those that have hurt us. Fear can be so paralyzing that when we are full of it, no matter how many connections we make in life it still feels lonely from the lack of self-*love* that we have.

One thing we know is that hurt people hurt people. When we are living in fear, it is easy for us to be negative and to always see the difficulties in most things because we have lost our confidence. It is painful to see anything in *love*.

We have conditioned ourselves for protection and to never trust others or ourselves because we live with a hurt that, most of the time something that we lost and also something we *loved*. With the belief that what we *loved* is now gone, we feel empty from *love*. If someone is living in fear and we are to put him or her in an uncomfortable position, whether it is mentally, physically, spiritually and even financially, they have a difficult time expressing and coping with the fact that they are not in control. When you poke a "bear" they will react and can very quickly hurt people from the perspective of self-protection, and not having to feel additional pain in their life. The hardest part about this stage is that no matter how much attention we give them or how much we gift them, there will always be a lack of fulfillment or satisfaction.

Some of the core reasons people live in fear:

- Having to live with the expectations of their family and friends
- Not having a true identity
- Fear of rejection
- Not being able to express your feelings and being understood
- Staying in a job that has an unhealthy environment
- Not wanting to hurt someone's feelings
- Getting hurt emotionally, financially, physically, and mentally
- And lots of other general phobias that people are afraid of, from living in fear.

Lion: Selfish

Having the courage to recognize that your life is filled with fear and choosing to change it is one of the hardest and bravest steps someone can take to regain the control of the life they have been living. I say control in a relative term because we ultimately can't control anything, but how we feel is within our control. It's a simple process of changing your thoughts, changing your feelings and that in turn changes our behaviors.

But when a person makes that choice to have a better life, it can be perceived by friends, family, and our leaders that we are living a selfish life because we are no longer being molded by the conditions and expectations that they expect us to remain in. It's a process of making choices to see what we like and what we don't like. Finding our true self. Once we continue living with our best intentions and living for ourselves, we realize that in order to find true peace we need to be selfless. Taking that step is the biggest step in choosing to live selflessly.

Horse: Non compromising

Living without compromising doesn't mean that we are continuing to live selfishly, but we realize that it is ok to say no to things that don't provide us happiness or that we don't want to genuinely do. When we make choices from the genuine care, we can live without resentment or expecting anything in return. By only making these choices we can live with pure peace and happiness because we are holding on to our own happiness. We also grow compassion for those that are still in the lower stages of growth and have the ability to stay in peace knowing that the people and things around us have to be accountable for what is balanced in everything.

Horses are known for being extremely balanced creatures. They are the only animal that can remain calm and focused when a person is riding in a competition or even in battle, but can be empathetic towards our emotions and can recognize the presence of fear. Because they have the ability to be balanced in times of fear and **love**. They are one of my favorite animals in the universe. Just a fun note that I enjoy is a group of horses is called a *team*.

"What do you believe?

(IF YOU DON'T BELIEVE IN SOMETHING, YOU WILL FALL FOR ANYTHING)

As a young kid I grew up in a typical Christian home. Life was very routine and the guidelines of our life was pretty much outlined for us. Waking up every Sunday to go to church and pray to God and Jesus Christ to forgive us of our sins and to remember the sacrifice that he made for our sins. With this belief, we had to make sure that we didn't allow the "devil" to influence us in making bad choices. And if we did, we would be living a life that was wrong. Some of those rules of the beliefs are:

- Not drinking alcohol
- Not listening to non-Christian music
- Making sure that we gave 10% of our income to the church
- Not fellowshipping with non-Christians
- Never using any bad words
- Accepting that we are only human and less than God and his creations
- Only fun that we should have needs to be holy and acceptable to the God we pray to
- That we should not have lust
- That we should not be gluttonous
- Never have a desire for greed
- Not be a sloth

- Never have wrath
- Not be envious
- And not have pride

I know that in the specific word alone these things are not good for humanity nor do they show compassion. Just as the word selfish needs to be redefined most of these "sins" are not wrong to have or want. But in the intent of why and how we want them is more important and can be good for our soul. Having a desire for greed is not good in the sense of happiness coming from the more money you have, but I think a word that can be parallel to that word with positive energy is *success*. Wanting to grow and be successful is good for the soul, but the perception from others not knowing the intent can be seen as greedy.

Another big issue I have with these beliefs is not fellowshipping with non-Christians. Saying that I can't associate with someone because they do not live with the rules that "I" do is very judgmental. I do believe that celebrating our similar purpose in that we are all human and different in our own ways is great. And making sure that we surround ourselves with people who believe *why* we believe what we believe is much more important than the actual belief itself.

If I am from India, and I only speak Hindi and my God is Muhammad or Ala, and I don't understand the English language from an American and their word for God is Jesus Christ in Christianity, we will never be able to communicate our true beliefs based on words or rules because of our own interpretation and perception. If we know *why* we believe what we believe and our intention is **love** and *compassion*, it really doesn't matter what someone calls their God and what rules they have. **Love** has no conditions or expectations.

Knowing that **love** is the intent in my life, I am able to see past someone's pain of not being understood is very easy once you have gone through the process of finding compassion in yourself. What I truly believe for myself is that the universe is made of energy, and that energy is *love*. I don't believe that we have evil in the world, but only a lack of *love*. If we can see from the perspective that the universe is always moving in *love*, we can see how the Universe always follows a pattern of *love*.

The grass is always green, the sun always rises and sets from east to west, eyes and ears are always on our head, what goes up must come down, and what hurts always builds strength. Just like after rain comes the rainbow and the harder you pull back on a bow and arrow the farther forward it will go. The patterns in the universe are from the intent of *love* and will always ensure Balance. Believing in patterns has allowed me to see things that can happen in the future. Not seeing the actual event, I know that the story never changes, but only the players do. Once you know your place in the universe, things start to align with your true desires and how your true authentic self-finds true happiness.

Togetherness

(THE JOURNEY OF A THOUSAND MILES, BEGINS WITH A SINGLE STEP)

Because I believe that we attract individuals similar to who we are, I know that the world of events and weddings started with innocence and it desperately needs redirection in almost every area of the market today. Taking responsibility in the superficial industry that it has become is the first step to find our way back to the days of events when we created events gathered in the presence of pure *love*.

Having done almost 50,000 events, it is very hard for me to remember even 1,000 of the couples and meeting planners that I had the pleasure and honor of working with. The process of contracting to the meetings when staying on deadlines to ensure all the details are perfect and reviewed is extremely fast and short-lived.

This process works for a numbers game and to impact the bottom line, but it does not grow connection, chemistry and most importantly, Loyalty. Working with most of the professionals today they even understand how intense the rat race of event planning really is. And that increases the handicap of the process.

So we understand that the industry has forgotten that we desire connection and the first thought we need to have to make that connection is understanding who we are, and what we believe. Once we take the time to develop our team and our brand, we can attract the likes of who we genuinely are. On a basic level, talking to each other is how we can discover who and what we are to our clients and couples, however, because the process is so short, it is easy for us to say all the right things after reading a couple by observing the way they walk, how they hold each other's hands.

The questions they ask will tell us who they are and what they want and desire for their wedding or event. This is good but the time it should take is different for every couple and should be for the event planner or leader. This can apply to how we hire our team as well. I believe that we should get to know the couple outside of a boardroom or a walkthrough, the environment that is only directing the immediate business transaction is hiding the other beliefs of our clients. I know that sharing a walk in a park or enjoying a meal together is a great way to start.

Meals and Drinks

Biting into an In-N-Out burger, hearing the sound of fresh cracking lettuce leaf and the crusted soft center bun, sends a shock of happiness into my soul. Because of that experience, I immediately see life a little brighter and warmer. I believe that any time we gather with someone and enjoy breaking of bread, a little bit of connection and a bond is built, from that moment. Food is a bridge of connection, and it's up to us to cross it. Being that we are pure energy, we require energy to maintain our bodies. When we look at the possibility for the belief that we are part of something more than just the fast food burger joint stuffing our faces to get us through the next few hours until we ingest another meaningless calorie value meal. Let me be clear. This is not my piece on natural and healthy eating, this is about me expressing that food is a moment that should be treasured because it feeds us so that we can continue to create and develop a connection with everything in this world. What we consumed had life and is part of the cycle of the world we live in.

I also believe that when a meal is prepared, it may not be made with the best, purest, or most expensive ingredients, but what I do know is that the secret ingredient to anything that we create is *love*.

The flavor of *love* and the impact it has on the food and

beverage we digest and partake of magically transforms the experience entirely.

One of my favorite dishes is Truffle Macaroni and Cheese. Granted, I know that Gordon Ramsey would be disturbed hearing me declare that this is a favorite dish of mine because of his disgust with truffle oil, not truffle itself, but the moment I enjoyed this dish for the first time had an impact on me that I won't forget. It is a Michael Mina signature dish and I was taking a professionalism class at the *Arcadia* restaurant private dining room when it was being served. I am very big on etiquette with confidence not on playing a part of being stuck up. So I was in *love* with the class and the little tricks and tips we were taught. Then I was enjoying this amazing dish with other professionals, and the way we took each bite and instantly tasted better just because of the company I was in and how we enjoyed it.

I think another example would be if I were a San Francisco Giants fan. The moment a child walks into the stadium with his father and is handed that foot-long Oscar Meyer. He takes a bite and instantly that becomes one of the happiest moments in that child's life, and he will never forget the day at the ballgame with his father.

I believe that food magnifies a connection because it reminds us to use our senses and that triggers memories after the moment has come and gone. So the importance for taking the time to enjoy and making the intention to be grateful for the food and its power to build a connection is priceless.

When interacting with a couple or a guest, we need to remember that at the core we are people, and the connection is what we are designed to make with our lives. So take the time and have the courage to spend the time and energy to create a meal for one another. Go to a local eatery or pub to share a milkshake or a bowl of nachos. These moments create intimacy, and intimacy is another level of connection That is what being human is all about! Food and beverage have history. Imagine what we would believe if the last supper of Christ were the last game of Cricket? It doesn't have the same amount of connection or relate-ability does it? I also think that when we drink an old fashion or a vodka martini extra dirty, we like to feel the connection to Frank Sinatra, James Bond, or even Audrey Hepburn. Never is it, "hey man, I wanna get fucked up until I can't feel my face!" We begin drinking because it has a social status privilege and significance. And we continue that tradition unknowing how much impact we have in gathering around a bottle of wine and a fireplace, or sangria on a beach coastline, or with a pint at our company holiday party. Whenever we are at a place of enjoyment, or a time that will change our lives, food and beverage will always be a staple in our moments.

Hobbies and Interests

So once we discover a little about ourselves, the desire to discover more increases daily. One way we can continue to feed our identity and our interests is to just do more, and push our limits and the abilities we have discovered and the ones we want to explore. At first, most of them will be related to community norms, like festivals or holiday festivities. But when you look deep inside yourself, you can feel the sensation to find, do, and be more. Trust your *gut*-life will do all the work in speaking to you.

It takes practicing confidence to be silent and listen to the voice inside you, your intuition, your core beliefs. They will tell you what the next direction your interests want to move towards. We live in a capitalist era where everything costs something and nothing is free. So we must find balance in our time, and in our hobbies and interests. It is just as important to have them as it is too not. Know when too and when to not have them. Maintaining balance in oneself is the ultimate identity.

Adventure

When I think of an adventure, I think of an exotic trip to the Amazon rainforest, backpacking the mountains and hiking up waterfalls that at a glance seem to be an illusion. A moment in time where work is no longer a priority nor are you wishing you would have a moment of silence away from the distractions. But instead, you are watching birds fly effortlessly from one branch to the next, embracing the essence of nature and anticipating your resort's bottomless drinks, and beautiful view from your suite. Oh, to be in the beautiful amazon.

It sounds like an adventure, and looks like one, and most certainly feels like one. But without a second more. I must add that this adventure would mean nothing without the fundamental understanding of why we do what we do. Let's take a crash course, we will call it a journey to an adventure.

I've always believed that our heart looks for three fundamental things -passion, adventure, and *love*. These fundamentals make for a better life. However, we lose the simple meaning of the three things that are the beginning essentials of life due to the fact that we are constantly living for the approval of another human. We miss it, we lose it like a slippery bar of soap!

If my parents approve of my career, I will go. If my friends set aside a weekend to take a trip to my destination of choice, I will go. And if they *love* me, I will *love* them. Nothing says I don't know what I want- more than the empty efforts given to another to in turn feel alive.

As children, we don't fear to find something new and not like it. It's slim and honestly very forgiving the way a child can live. Children will run full speed down a hill with no anticipation of a fall but with no hesitation will make their way down. Full of joy and innocent laughter.

As we grow up, we find a gap between wanting freedom and having already learned disappointment, fear, anxiety. It's unfortunate to know that life can strip us down of that child we knew would ride that rollercoaster over and over until feeling dizzy and or run down that hill full speed.

Many years ago I watched a man pick himself up after losing his family and two businesses, watching him look into his future and saying, "I've learned a lot about what can go wrong, but this is the chance to endure, practice the things life teaches us about the journey into life". What can go right and will I be ok with what will go wrong? Tragedy, triggers, trauma are responsible for our lack of risk taking.

Our first and effortless step taken into the world of adventure is to let go of the fear that has clogged the lifeline of childlike faith. The type of faith that is certain every little thing will be ok. Let go of fear, and hold on to acceptance, of nothing less than yourself.

Adventures are the kinds we face when we are alone in our thoughts, the pleasures we find guilty and true for ourselves. Our adventures are lived during the exact moment we do something consciously to create a life we want. With risks, with challenges, with everything that was intended to destroy your last bit of hope. These are what is making and molding your life to be that adventure your heart craves and by the time we see the finished product, we would already have lived it. The irony of it all is that we never truly enjoy the journey if we don't first learn to get out of our own way and let life unfold before our naked eye.

Overthinking is destructive and is not a safe way to live life. It's fear saying you can and will control the things -"Learning is like healing it happens over time."

The steps taken into a new life hold more than just a step, a step forward sometimes it requires you to take a glance to your past. Healing from the memories and failed attempts at an adventurous life. A glance into your past to realize that what continues to tell us that we are not able to fill the shoes of those who were courageous, think of those moments where true and authentic vulnerability is of the essence. But you bombed! Everybody bombs!

Now in the simplest of ways. Admit to the faults that may have hurt another, that damaged you because you bombed. This, ladies and gentlemen, is the beginning of a transformation in your mind to give your new adventure space to be free, to grow and be strong and brave.

To be Continued…

ABOUT THE AUTHOR

Eric has been in hospitality for 20 years and owns a business development company, The Chef Hero, that teaches startups and struggling outdated business leaders the value to innovate and create positive experiences for the people that support them.

Eric's past experience of owning a luxury full service event center, two restaurants, and a celebrity wedding planning and design company, has brought him to China, Hong Kong, Taiwan, Mexico and all over the United States. Eric lives in Northern California and has two wonderful young sons.

Made in the USA
Middletown, DE
11 October 2022